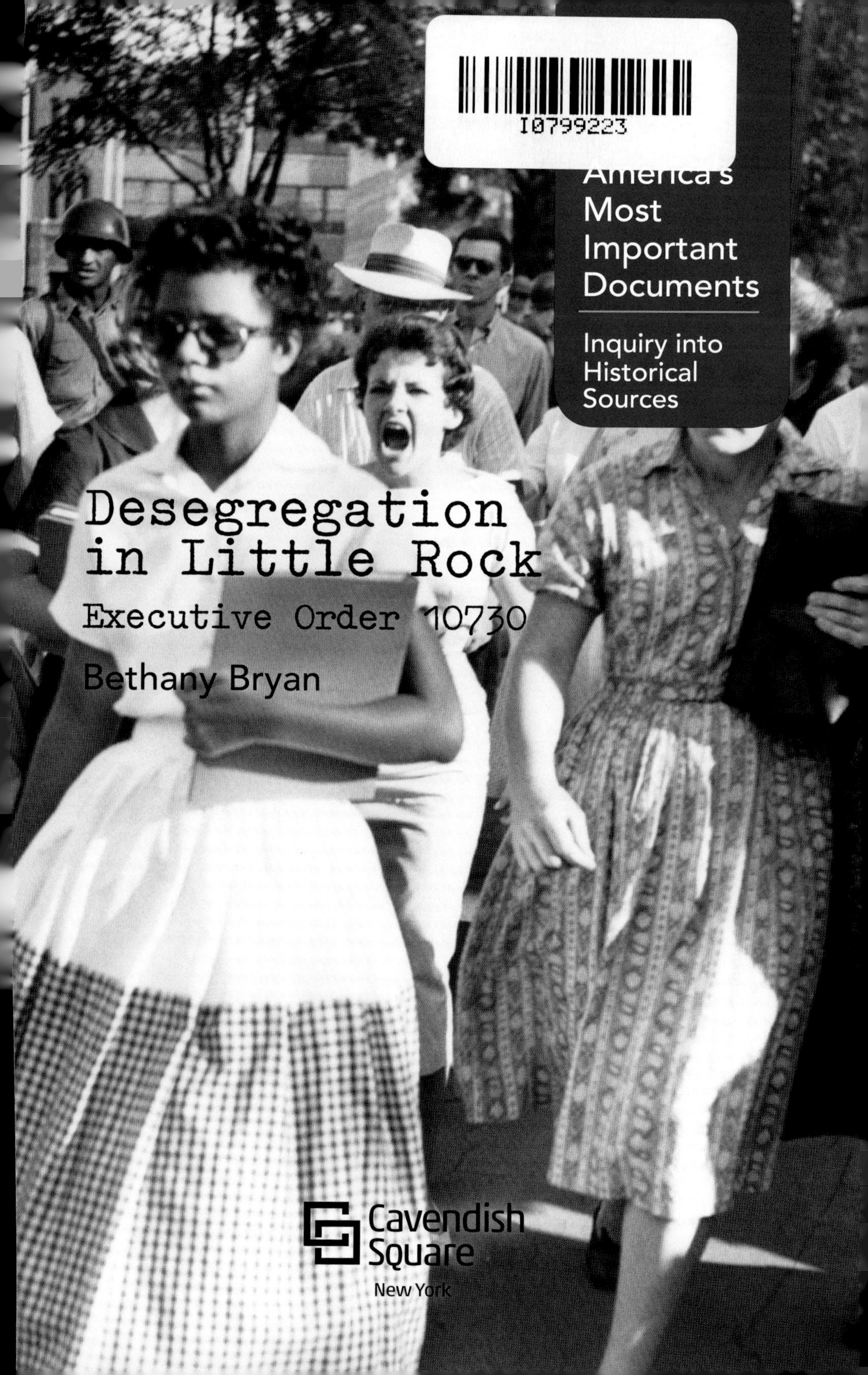

America's Most Important Documents

Inquiry into Historical Sources

Desegregation in Little Rock

Executive Order 10730

Bethany Bryan

Cavendish Square
New York

Published in 2019 by Cavendish Square Publishing, LLC
243 5th Avenue, Suite 136, New York, NY 10016

First Edition

Library of Congress Cataloging-in-Publication Data

Names: Bryan, Bethany, author.
Title: Desegregation in Little Rock : executive order 10730 / Bethany Bryan.
Description: First edition. | New York, NY : Cavendish Square Publishing, LLC, 2019. | Series: America's most important documents: inquiry into historical sources | Includes bibliographical references and index. | Audience: Grades 5-8.
Identifiers: LCCN 2018002860 (print) | LCCN 2018005231 (ebook) | ISBN 9781502636171 (ebook) | ISBN 9781502636164 (library bound) | ISBN 9781502636188 (pbk)
Subjects: LCSH: School integration--Arkansas--Little Rock--History--20th century. | African American students--Arkansas--Little Rock--History--20th century. | Central High School (Little Rock, Ark.)--History. | Segregation--United States--History. | United States--Race relations--History.
Classification: LCC LC214.23.L56 (ebook) | LCC LC214.23. L56 B78 2019 (print) | DDC 379.2/630976773--dc23
LC record available at https://lccn.loc.gov/2018002860

Editorial Director: David McNamara
Editor: Kristen Susienka
Copy Editor: Alex Tessman
Associate Art Director: Amy Greenan
Designer: Joe Parenteau
Production Coordinator: Karol Szymczuk
Photo Research: J8 Media

The photographs in this book are used by permission and through the courtesy of: Cover, 4, 7, 41 Bettmann/Getty Images; p. 8 Library of Congress/Wikimedia Commons/File:J. S. Smith & Co. copy of the Emancipation Proclamation.jpg/Public Domain; p. 10 Universal History Archive/UIG/Getty Images; p. 12 Everett Historical/Shutterstock.com; p. 14 William Lovelace/Express/Hulton Archive/Getty Images; p. 15 North Wind Picture Archives; p. 17 Jose Gil/Shutterstock.com; p. 18 Carl Iwasaki/The LIFE Images Collection/Getty Images; p. 20 Galerie Bilderwelt/Getty Images; p. 23 Topical Press Agency/Getty Images; p. 26 George Silk/The LIFE Picture Collection/Getty Images; p. 28 Archive PL/Alamy Stock Photo; p. 29 Francis Miller/The LIFE Picture Collection/Getty Images; p. 32 Hulton Archive/Getty Images; p. 34 Buyenlarge/Getty Images; p. 36 Keystone-France/Gamma-Keystone/Getty Images; p. 40 Pictorial Press Ltd/Alamy Stock Photo; p. 42 Adam Jones, Ph.D./Wikimedia Commons/File:Facade of Central High School Little Rock Arkansas USA 01.jpg/CC BY SA 3.0; p. 45 PhotoQuest/Getty Images; p. 46 Corbis/Getty Images; p. 48 Mitch Potter/Toronto Star/Getty Images; p. 51 Joe Scarnici/Getty Images; p. 53 Frazer Harrison/Getty Images.

Printed in the United States of America

Contents

Chapter One

A History of Segregation

The Declaration of Independence, one of the United States' first founding documents, was written in 1776. It says that "all men are created equal." However, since that time, one question comes up again and again: What does that really mean? Were all people really created equal in the eyes of the Founding Fathers? Or was this line of text referring only to men—particularly white men, like the Founding Fathers themselves?

When the Declaration of Independence was written, the African slave trade was booming, bringing tens of thousands of enslaved African people to the American colonies each year. By 1860, there were 3.9 million slaves living in the United States. When slavery was at last abolished in 1865, equal rights were not automatically granted to former slaves. They often struggled

Opposite: The Declaration of Independence was signed by the Founding Fathers on July 4, 1776, promising equal rights to all men.

with disease and starvation. Many died as a result. During and after Reconstruction of the South following the Civil War, several state legislatures passed laws that would effectively keep black and white citizens separated in schools, public transportation, at drinking fountains, in bathrooms, and at other public places. Those who opposed these laws felt that they violated the idea of "all men being created equal." Many who supported these laws said that the services were equal, just kept separate.

In the 1950s and 1960s, more people started to take action. The civil rights movement that developed during these decades was a turning point in the United States. Separate was not equal, and the fight for equal rights was about to begin.

A History of Slavery

The first slaves were brought from Africa to the American colonies in 1619, and the practice expanded throughout the Northern and Southern colonies over the next two centuries. As time went by, slavery became a cornerstone to the economy of the Southern colonies. This area was dominated by large farms, or plantations, that grew massive amounts of crops for export. One of the most important crops in the South during that time was tobacco. In order to keep up with the demand of exporting to Great Britain and other European countries, where tobacco use had grown in popularity, Southern farmers relied on slave labor. Slavery existed in the North as well, but it was not as central to the economy.

Over time, an abolitionist movement called for the end of the practice of slavery. Slowly, it spread in the North until states began to outlaw the practice, starting with Vermont in 1777. Soon, Northern states and Southern states were at

In the Southern states, cotton was king. It required a lot of manpower to grow and produce, and this work was done by slaves.

odds over the practice of slavery. As the United States began to expand westward into the land acquired by the Louisiana Purchase in 1803, Americans in the North and South began to question whether or not slavery should be allowed in the new states. If abolition spread to the new states, it could jeopardize the practice of slavery in the South. This conflict came to a head in 1861—in response to abolitionist Abraham Lincoln being elected president—when the states of South Carolina, Mississippi, Florida, Alabama, Georgia, Louisiana, Texas, Virginia, Arkansas, North Carolina, and Tennessee withdrew from the Union. The result was the outbreak of the Civil War.

The Emancipation Proclamation

At the beginning of the Civil War, the main goal of the North was to preserve the Union by bringing the Confederate states back into the country, not to necessarily abolish slavery. But

The Emancipation Proclamation was not only a morally sound decision. Lincoln believed that it was also a strong military strategy, if slaves fled to the North and joined the Union army.

after a few years, this plan evolved. Thousands of slaves were fleeing to the Northern states and joining the Union cause. Noticing this, Abraham Lincoln saw an opportunity to help the Union by calling for an emancipation, or freeing, of the slaves in the Confederate states, hoping that this action would convince some of the Southern states to give up their cause. The Emancipation Proclamation was an executive order—a written order, calling for action, from the sitting president that bypasses congressional approval—issued early in 1863.

The order began:

> *[O]n the first day of January, in the year of our Lord one thousand eight hundred and sixty-three, all persons held as slaves within any State or designated part of a State, the people whereof shall then be in rebellion against the United States, shall be then, thenceforward, and forever free; and the Executive Government of the United States, including the military and naval authority thereof, will recognize and maintain the freedom of such persons, and will do no act or acts to repress such persons, or any of them, in any efforts they may make for their actual freedom.*

Although not a single slave was able to walk free when the proclamation was issued—because the Confederacy operated under its own government—this order changed the tide of the war in favor of the Union. The Civil War became a fight for freedom. The Confederate states, which exported cotton to France and England, looked to Europe for allies, but found none because no country wanted to appear pro-slavery in the face of the practice's waning popularity.

In the end, the Confederacy struggled to provide enough supplies to outfit an army. There simply wasn't enough money in the Confederate treasury to finance a war. Soldiers were injured and struggled to find basic necessities like food and clothing. On

General Robert E. Lee and General Ulysses S. Grant met on April 9, 1865, to discuss the terms of the Southern army's surrender.

April 9, 1865, Confederate general Robert E. Lee surrendered to General Ulysses S. Grant. The Thirteenth Amendment, formally abolishing slavery, was passed by Congress on January 31, 1865, and ratified (officially added to the Constitution) on December 6, 1865. The era of slavery in the United States was over. Abraham Lincoln called for a reconstruction of the South and a plan for unity, saying in his second inaugural address, "With malice toward none; with charity for all."

Johnson's Reconstruction and the Radical Republicans

The Civil War was over, but that didn't mean an end to racism and discrimination. After the assassination of Abraham Lincoln in April 1865, there was a new president in office: former vice president Andrew Johnson. Johnson's approach to Reconstruction was quite different from Lincoln's original plan. Originally from Tennessee, Johnson was more sympathetic to the

Southern states than Lincoln had been, even though he had sided with the Union during the Civil War. He had supported slavery during his time in Congress in the 1840s and 1850s, only revising his opinion once Southern leaders began to call for secession. He was the only senator from the South who supported the Union and even spoke out against secession while traveling around his home state in the early 1860s. His Southern roots made him a good running mate for Abraham Lincoln, as many believed that he would help heal the breach between the Northern and Southern states.

And Furthermore

A few days after the surrender by the South, Abraham Lincoln was attending a performance of the play *Our American Cousin* at Ford's Theatre in Washington, DC, with his wife Mary Todd, when he was shot in the back of the head by Confederate sympathizer John Wilkes Booth. Lincoln died at 7:22 a.m. on April 15, 1865.

After he was sworn in as president, Andrew Johnson granted amnesty to many former Confederates and gave his permission for the Southern states to hold elections. Almost immediately, Southern governments voted in policies that would continue to restrict the freedoms of former slaves. Before Lincoln's death, Congress had created the Freedmen's Bureau, an organization that would help provide food, shelter, clothing, medicine, and land to Southerners, both white and black, affected or displaced by the Civil War. But the bureau was not well funded from the beginning and faced a great deal of opposition from Southern whites who did not support the president. Many questioned how much support should be provided and for how long. Attempts by antislavery "Radical" Republicans to improve the reach of the bureau were thwarted by President Johnson, citing that he believed that the Freedmen's Bureau violated states' rights and created a financial burden on American citizens. The organization finally folded to pressure in 1872. During its short life, the bureau did fund the building of over one thousand schools, including a few historically black colleges that remain in operation today.

Antislavery activist Frederick Douglass once wrote of Andrew Johnson, "Whatever Andrew Johnson may be, he is no friend of our race." Johnson was not a popular president, as Reconstruction policy clashes with the Radical Republican-majority Congress continued through the rest of his presidency. He suspended Secretary of War Edwin Stanton, who did not agree with his policies, resulting in impeachment proceedings by the House of Representatives under the Tenure of Office Act. Johnson was eventually acquitted, but he did not run for reelection in 1886. With Johnson's relationship with Congress in shambles, the United States entered into a period of "Radical Reconstruction," in which Congress worked to undo some of the president's damaging policies by overriding his veto powers.

Andrew Johnson, circa 1860. He became president in 1865.

In 1866, Congress passed the first Civil Rights Act. Under this bill, all people born in the United States would be granted citizenship (although this did not apply to Native Americans).

In 1867, Congress passed the Reconstruction Act, again bypassing President Johnson's authority. This law imposed specific terms on the Southern states and how they would be readmitted to the Union. The South (except for Tennessee) was temporarily divided into five military districts, and each state was required to write a new state constitution to be approved by a majority of state voters. All Southern states had to also ratify the Thirteenth and Fourteenth Amendments—abolishing slavery and granting citizenship to former slaves, respectively. Arkansas was the first state to comply and was readmitted to the Union on June 22, 1868. Georgia was the last Southern state to rejoin the Union, on July 15, 1870.

Hero of the Civil War Ulysses S. Grant won the presidential election of 1868, and although he was not a Radical Republican, he allowed the Radical Reconstruction to continue. Andrew Johnson returned home to Tennessee, but his approach to Southern Reconstruction would continue to haunt the United States and its citizens for the next century.

Jim Crow Laws

The Reconstruction period ended around 1877, and although the former Confederate states had rejoined the Union, Reconstruction had not fixed everything. Civil rights legislation passed at the national level was often useless against state laws. In many states, certain laws were passed in an attempt to restrict the lives and freedoms of former slaves and their families. These restrictive laws passed in the years after Reconstruction came to be called the "Jim Crow laws." Named after a minstrel show character of the same name, "Jim Crow" was derogatory slang for an African American man. These

This sign was erected in Mississippi because of the Jim Crow laws. Many defended these laws as "separate but equal" in the eyes of the law.

policies didn't just pass in the South, but in a majority of the United Sates. Essentially, the Jim Crow laws established separate rules for black people and white people. They called for separation by race, establishing separate bathrooms, drinking fountains, train cars, and other restrictions of public resources.

In Alabama it was illegal for black and white people to occupy the same dining room in a restaurant. Marriage between races was illegal in many states. Black people were not allowed to be buried in cemeteries designated for white people in the state of Georgia. In North Carolina, black schools and white schools were not allowed to use the same textbooks. In South Carolina, textile factory workers of different races could not work in the same room, use the same entrance, or even look through the same windows. Businesses could choose to not hire black workers at all.

The United States went into a depression in the late 1890s because of an agricultural crisis that swept the South and plains states. Farmers were simply producing too much, and the crops were losing value. Railroads began to go bankrupt. Unemployment was at 19 percent. One of the most convenient scapegoats for the depression was black people, often blamed for "taking jobs" from poor whites. Newspapers helped to play into the bias by focusing crime reporting on black people who had committed crimes, even making up stories at times.

Even after the Fifteenth Amendment gave black men the right to vote, state legislatures across the United States created policies to prevent them from actually voting, requiring poll taxes and reading tests. Others were threatened and intimidated until they were afraid to cast a vote.

Other black people were simply murdered. Between 1877 and 1940, around four thousand black people were lynched, many by members of the Ku Klux Klan. These actions were often justified by it being the "Lord's will" that blacks be eliminated in order to keep the white race "pure."

This illustration shows black men voting after the passing of the Fifteenth Amendment.

Plessy v. Ferguson

In 1870, the first Civil Rights Act was brought before the Senate by Massachusetts senator Charles Sumner. The act guaranteed all citizens, regardless of race, the right to access things like theaters, public schools, churches, and the like. And then Sumner passed away suddenly of a heart attack in 1874, before the bill could be voted into law a year later. Without its strongest advocate, the Civil Rights Act of 1870 was stripped of references to integrated education and rendered ineffective as a piece of legislation. In 1883, it was declared unconstitutional, as the Supreme Court did not feel that Congress should have the authority to impose discrimination laws upon private businesses and individuals.

And Furthermore

A key leader in civil rights was Ida B. Wells. She became a journalist and activist in 1884. She worked to introduce anti-lynching legislation at a national level, although all were blocked by Southern senators and never became law. Ida B. Wells would go on to cofound the National Association for the Advancement of Colored People (NAACP).

In 1892, a man named Homer Plessy boarded a train. Plessy was a member of the Citizens' Committee to Test the Constitutionality of the Separate Car Law, a group of men who hoped to overturn a Louisiana state law that called for "separate but equal" train car accommodations. Plessy was one-eighth black and therefore light-skinned, but in boarding and taking a seat in the "whites-only" car, he was technically in violation of the law, which the Citizens' Committee believed violated the Thirteenth Amendment. Plessy was quickly arrested and thrown in jail, and the group hired attorney Albion Tourgée to represent them in a lawsuit they hoped would help overturn the law. But it was decided by the Supreme Court that as long as the accommodations were equal, the individual states could continue to enforce segregation laws. "Separate but equal" would be the law of the land for the next sixty years.

This plaque stands at the tomb of Homer Plessy.

Brown v. Board of Education

In the 1950s, the NAACP was working to bring lawsuits against school districts that continued to enforce segregation in schools. The most famous of these cases, and the one that gave a landmark victory to the civil rights movement, was *Brown v. Board of Education of Topeka*. It was this Supreme Court decision that finally turned the tide for segregation in schools.

In *Plessy v. Ferguson*, it was decided that the federal government could do nothing to fight discrimination committed by privately funded businesses. However, state-funded schools were a different matter. According to the Virginia Historical Society, schools for black students often did not receive the kind of funding that schools for white students did. There were fewer books, conditions of schoolrooms were worse, and black teachers were paid less. Black students did not receive the quality of education that white students did.

From left to right, Vicki Henderson, Donald Henderson, Linda Brown, James Emanuel, Nancy Todd, and Katherine Cooper were represented in the *Brown v. Board of Education of Topeka* case.

Many black parents were unhappy with the education their children were receiving. One of these parents was Oliver Brown, whose daughter, Linda, was turned away from attending a white school in Topeka, Kansas, in the early 1950s. Brown began to explore ways to legally challenge these segregation laws.

Although Brown's is the name on the class-action lawsuit, it actually represented the Brown case and four other similar cases. The plaintiffs were represented by an attorney named Thurgood Marshall, a longtime civil rights activist. Marshall would go on to become the first African American justice of the Supreme Court.

Early in the Supreme Court's hearing of the case, then Chief Justice Fred Vinson argued for upholding *Plessy v. Ferguson*, but then Vinson died suddenly and was replaced with Earl Warren. The new chief justice didn't agree with the "separate but equal" doctrine, and so he worked to sway the other justices

The Final Push: The Montgomery Bus Boycott

On December 1, 1955, a longtime civil rights activist named Rosa Parks was on her way home from work. The "whites only" section of the bus was full, and so when a white man boarded the bus and demanded a seat, the driver asked black riders sitting in the front row of the "black section" at the rear of the bus to give up their seats to white passengers. Parks refused and was arrested.

On December 5, Parks went to court and was found guilty of violating segregation laws and was fined $10 (about $91 today). On that day, black citizens of Montgomery, Alabama, began a boycott of the city's bus system until the city agreed to abolish segregation on public transportation.

The boycott drew media attention to the city of Montgomery. Dr. Martin Luther King Jr. was elected president of the newly founded Montgomery Improvement Association. Violence broke out as tensions rose. Black churches and the homes of black leaders were bombed by the KKK. Parks herself lost her job and faced harassment and threats. She and her family finally relocated to Detroit, Michigan.

Finally, on November 13, 1956, the Supreme Court ruled segregation on public transportation unconstitutional.

toward integration. On May 17, 1954, the Supreme Court issued its decision. Black students were being "deprived of the equal protection of the laws guaranteed by the Fourteenth Amendment." *Plessy v. Ferguson* was overturned. Schools were going to be integrated across the United States.

Chapter Two

Executive Order 10730

Integrating American schools was never going to be a simple task. While many were in support of the progress being made, others were opposed—in some parts of the country, those opposed made up the majority and were in positions of power. But the Supreme Court's ruling on *Brown v. Board* was law. Therefore, the country needed the ability to enforce this law. One of these ways was through the authority of the president, Dwight Eisenhower.

Eisenhower's Rise to President

Dwight D. Eisenhower was born on October 14, 1890, in Denison, Texas. However, he spent his childhood growing up in Abilene,

Opposite: Long before he was president, Dwight Eisenhower was supreme commander of the Allied forces during World War II.

The Republican Party Divides

The Republican Party of 1952, which elected Eisenhower as their presidential candidate, was not the Republican Party of 1860 that had elected Abraham Lincoln. The original Republican Party was founded in the mid-1850s, their main platform to abolish slavery. At the beginning of the twentieth century, however, the party found itself divided between progressive Republican Theodore Roosevelt and conservative Republican William Howard Taft, over business reform.

During his time in office—from 1901 to 1909—Roosevelt supported regulations that helped prevent monopolies and exploitation of workers. By 1910, Roosevelt was glad to hand over the reins of the presidency to his friend and former secretary of war, Taft, trusting that this work would continue.

Although Taft worked hard in the beginning, he soon aligned himself with more conservative members of the party, eventually backing away from the "trust-busting"

Kansas. After graduating from high school, Dwight, often called Ike, worked to help pay for his brother's college tuition before being sent to West Point, New York, to train at the US Military Academy. Right before Eisenhower was to be sent to Europe to fight alongside Allied forces during World War I, the war ended. Over the next several years, he served as a military aide to both General John J. Pershing and Douglas MacArthur.

policies of his predecessor. In frustration, Roosevelt left the Republican Party and founded the Bull Moose Party, named because Roosevelt felt he was as tough as a moose. Many progressive Republicans followed Roosevelt in leaving the party. Since then, the Republican Party has followed a more conservative ideology. Republicans of Eisenhower's era, however, were still progressive for their time, supporting a higher minimum wage, unemployment insurance, and social security benefits.

Theodore Roosevelt (*left*) and William Howard Taft (*right*) had been friends and allies.

He was stationed for several years in the Philippines. Then, in 1941, World War II broke out.

Dwight Eisenhower was made a full general in 1943. Later that year he was named supreme commander of the Allied Expeditionary Force, giving him the task of planning the US invasion of Europe, which had slowly been taken over by Nazi forces. Under Eisenhower's command, Allied forces rose to victory in 1945. The Allied forces invaded Germany in December 1944, and Nazi Germany surrendered in January 1945. Dwight D. Eisenhower, who had grown up on the wrong side of the tracks in a small Kansas town, was a certified war hero.

In June 1952, Eisenhower retired from the military and joined the presidential race. People "liked Ike." He was affable and represented the everyman, and he promised to put an end to the Korean War, which had been waging since 1950. Eisenhower was a favorite for the Republican nomination. He won easily and became the thirty-fourth president of the United States.

During his presidency, Ike made good on his promise to end the Korean War as well as faced two immense challenges: the Cold War with the Soviet Union and the early years of the civil rights movement. Eisenhower was president during *Brown v. Board of Education of Topeka* and responded to the ruling by saying, "The Supreme Court has spoken and I am sworn to uphold the constitutional processes in this country; and I will obey." Many believe that this response did not show a firm support of school integration and civil rights, but simply a resigned acceptance. But whether or not President Eisenhower was an ally of equal rights, his actions over his eight years in office helped to shape future civil rights policies.

Integration in Progress

The *Brown v. Board of Education of Topeka* decision was poised to move the nation forward, but not everyone in the United States at the time was ready for progress. According to the Teaching Tolerance website, in 1956 only 15 percent of Southerners believed that black students and white students should attend the same schools. In the North, that number was 61 percent.

After the Supreme Court ruling, many school districts simply refused to integrate students. Others pursued further action in the courts to avoid integration. Segregationists argued that the US Constitution didn't require that black students and white students be integrated, and therefore it should be left up to the states to decide. In many states, segregation was simply "customary"—it was what they had always known, and felt uncomfortable with change. Many believed that black students wouldn't be able to keep up in white classrooms, operating under a long-perpetuated falsehood that black students simply weren't as intelligent.

Over the next five years, federal judges held desegregation hearings for more than two hundred schools. In May 1955, the Supreme Court issued a second opinion on *Brown v. Board of Education of Topeka*, which required schools to desegregate "with all deliberate speed." Riots broke out as white citizens attempted to block desegregation actions in Tennessee. In Virginia, many schools closed to avoid integration.

The Little Rock Nine

In Little Rock, Arkansas, in 1957, schools were still not integrated, but the school board had developed a plan to gradually desegregate the schools, starting in September of that year with Little Rock high schools. Elementary schools would follow soon after. This would make Little Rock the first Southern city to adhere to the *Brown v. Board of Education of Topeka* ruling. However, any black student to set foot in a formerly all-white school was going to face a lot of adversity and resistance.

The Arkansas state legislature had passed laws in February 1957 that worked to undermine the plan for integration. These

Under the protection of the National Guard and members of the military, the Little Rock Nine are shown here approaching Central High.

bills funneled state funds into the fight against integration and made it so that students were no longer required to attend integrated schools. These laws gave segregationists, including the Arkansas governor Orval Faubus, a legal foothold to continue to fight the Supreme Court ruling.

So a plan was formed to help the first days of integration go as smoothly and as safely as possible. Nine African American students were chosen by Arkansas NAACP president Daisy Bates to be the first to attend Little Rock's Central High School. Their names were Elizabeth Eckford, Minnijean Brown, Thelma Mothershed, Melba Patillo, Gloria Ray, Terrence Roberts, Jefferson Thomas, Carlotta Walls, and Ernest Green. These students attended counseling sessions to help them prepare for any hostility they might encounter. This group became known in the press as "the Little Rock Nine."

But as the first day of school approached, Arkansas governor Orval Faubus announced his intention to block the students' entry to the school by calling in the National Guard. He was supported by a number of groups, including the Capital Citizens Council and the Mother's League of Central High School. He justified his actions by saying that he was simply trying to avoid the violence and bloodshed. The students arrived at the school on September 4 to find their entry blocked by the Arkansas National Guard, along with a mob of angry white protestors, including fellow high school students, their parents, and other members of the community.

Elizabeth Eckford, who wasn't aware that all the students would be arriving together and therefore arrived alone, shared in a later account that a protestor spat on her as she approached the school. When she tried to pass through a line of soldiers, they blocked her path. There was nothing the students could do that morning but return home. Over the next several hours, rioters had beaten reporters and caused damage to the school.

Eisenhower's Reaction

When news of Governor Faubus's plans to block students from entering the school reached Washington, DC, on September 3, President Eisenhower was not pleased. For months, Congress had been working to pass the Civil Rights Act of 1957. Having passed in the House and Senate, the bill simply awaited Eisenhower's signature in order to become law. This bill would aid in the fight for equal voting rights for African Americans. Passing the bill had been a long, exhausting struggle, and Eisenhower really wanted to take a vacation. He was hoping to head to his home in Rhode Island for some time off when the news from Little Rock arrived. The Arkansas governor's rebellion not only violated the Supreme Court ruling, but it was also a huge personal inconvenience for the president.

Arkansas governor Orval Faubus addresses the public.

Eisenhower also wasn't terribly comfortable with handling civil rights issues. He frequently remarked, "You cannot change people's hearts merely by laws," when confronted with questions about the issue. At a news conference on September 3, when the president was expected to address the issue in Little Rock, he simply said that he was conferring with his attorney general, Herbert Brownell. The following day, Brownell announced that the federal government would be launching an investigation into Faubus's claims that integration would result in an outbreak of violence in Little Rock.

A Court Ruling

Ronald Davies was a federal judge from North Dakota. As the plan for school integration got under way in Arkansas, Judge Davies was called in to help, as the backlog of cases was getting overwhelming for the Arkansas judges. According to some comments Davies made several years later, in 1987, he didn't know what case he would be handling when he arrived in Arkansas. He was simply going because it was his duty as a federal judge. When the Little Rock Nine were denied access to Central High, Davies began legal proceedings against the Arkansas governor, ordering an injunction—essentially a court order that required that Faubus cease interfering with the integration process or face arrest, fines, or prison time. In total, Davies ordered the school to carry out the plan for integration three times.

Ronald Davies appears in his courtroom.

On September 5, the day after the students were denied access to the school, President Eisenhower sent a stern telegram to Governor Faubus, ordering him to allow the students to enter the school. "When I became President," the telegram read, "I took an oath to support and defend the Constitution of the United States. The only assurance I can give you is that the Federal Constitution will be upheld by me by every legal means at my command." Faubus continued to refuse the order to comply, insisting that he feared an outbreak of violence.

On September 11, Arkansas congressman Brooks Hays made a call to his friend Sherman Adams, who worked as one of the president's aides. His plan was to arrange a one-on-one meeting between Governor Faubus and the president. Eisenhower was in Rhode Island on vacation, but agreed to the meeting. The meeting took place on September 14 at the White House. During this discussion, Eisenhower suggested that Faubus could maintain the National Guard's presence at the school but change their orders to simply keeping the peace. The governor agreed, but when he returned to Little Rock, Faubus did not change his orders to the National Guard at all. Days later, on September 20, after appearing in Judge Davies's court, he completely dismissed the troops—probably to prove that an outbreak of violence was inevitable—and the nine African American students were allowed to enter the school. But they were also left unprotected. Violence broke out, and that day, the Little Rock Nine were evacuated from Central High by noon.

For a governor to refuse not only a federal judge's ruling, but also the direct order of a president is considered by many to be a treasonous offense. To continue to do so signified a breakdown of the government. A more serious action would need to be taken.

Executive Orders Explained

The first executive order was issued by George Washington in 1789, more of a request in those days than an order. He needed advice on taxation. He wrote several letters to his contemporaries, asking for them, "to impress me with a full, precise, and distinct general idea of the affairs of the United States." At the time, and up until the presidency of Abraham Lincoln, these actions weren't really considered "orders." They were often inconsequential. John Quincy Adams issued an executive order on July 11, 1826, enacting a day of mourning honoring the July 4 deaths of John Adams and Thomas Jefferson (the former presidents had died on the same day). By the president's order, the American flag would be lowered to half-mast and, "At early dawn thirteen guns shall be fired, and at intervals of thirty minutes between the rising and setting sun a single cannon will be discharged, and at the close of the day twenty-four rounds." When President Andrew Jackson left office in 1837, incoming president Martin Van Buren issued an executive order that since his predecessor was in ill health upon leaving office, he would be accompanied by a doctor as he traveled back to his home in Tennessee. The Emancipation Proclamation of 1863 was one of the first executive orders that really affected policy. Since then, executive orders tend to carry more weight.

Today, an executive order is essentially a directive from the president that bypasses Congress. These are often issued during times of crisis when Congress wouldn't usually have time to act. During World War II, President Roosevelt issued several executive orders. The most controversial and well known of these was executive order 9066—issued February 19, 1942—which forced Japanese Americans into internment camps out of fears that they were spies for the Japanese government. Over 110,000 Japanese American people were forced into camps and endured poor living conditions and treatment for the next two

The internment camp shown here housed Japanese American people during World War II.

and a half years. Roosevelt finally suspended the order and the detainees were released. During the war, Roosevelt also issued executive orders that would aid in the procurement of materials needed for the war effort and establishing a wartime workweek of forty-eight hours.

Executive orders are also sometimes issued if Congress is taking too long to act or refuses to act on a certain issue. For example, President Barack Obama issued executive order 13653 on November 1, 2013, to create programs and help the United States prepare for climate change. Climate change had long been a polarizing issue in Congress, and the president and other members of the Democratic Party felt that something needed to be done. This type of executive order is often controversial because many feel that it demonstrates an overreach of the executive branch.

The only thing that Congress can do if an executive order is unwise or damaging is pass legislation that counters it. This can take time and requires a majority vote. The courts can also intervene if the executive order appears to violate the Constitution, as happened with executive order 13769, issued by President Donald Trump, which banned entry to the US by citizens of Iran, Iraq, Libya, Somalia, Sudan, Syria, and Yemen, in an attempt to keep international terrorists from entering the country. Within days, the travel ban was blocked by the courts.

And Furthermore

President Franklin D. Roosevelt holds the record for the most executive issues ordered during his time in office at 3,721, while the least—none—were issued by William Henry Harrison—probably because Harrison fell sick and died after only thirty-one days in office.

Executive orders sometimes have positive outcomes, while others have consequences. However, not issuing an executive order might result in disaster or loss of life in certain situations. When used judiciously, executive orders play an important role in government.

Eisenhower Issues an Order

The president had tried negotiating with the Arkansas governor, meeting with him personally to try to come to an agreement. He had asked the courts to intervene. Nothing was helping convince Faubus that he needed to comply.

On September 23, a mob of around 1,500 individuals was gathered outside of Central High again, when four African American reporters were confronted by white protestors. Two

Martin Luther King Jr. (*right center*) led a march from Selma to Montgomery, Alabama, in March 1965 to aid in the fight for voting rights.

of the reporters were attacked, and while the crowd was focused on the melee, eight of the black students were finally able to enter the school through a side door. (The ninth student was chased away and was able to escape to safety, but the man accompanying him was beaten.) At last, the mayor of Little Rock sent an urgent telegram to the president, begging for him to intervene.

Eisenhower hadn't dealt more directly with the issue in Little Rock for a number of reasons. One of the most important reasons is that the president liked being liked. Taking action against a state governor would certainly be a divisive act. Since the Civil War, it would be a controversial act to send military troops into a Southern state. The president was also very cautious, after his years of military service. He was not impulsive. Decisions that Eisenhower made were made after he conferred with his staff and, since Eisenhower had always been religious, trusted members of the clergy—he called Reverend

Billy Graham to ask for advice, and Graham advised him to send in troops. The president also hoped that after a month of fruitless struggle, the Arkansas governor would give in to pressure. He didn't. At last, President Eisenhower agreed to sign an executive order, one that would send in the National Guard to protect the Little Rock Nine as they entered the school.

Dwight D. Eisenhower's executive order 10730 is not a long document. It also isn't an immediately recognizable document in the way the Declaration of Independence or the Emancipation Proclamation is. But it was and continues to be an important document in the history of the civil rights movement, as well as the history of the United States.

What Executive Order 10730 Says

By not complying with the Supreme Court's decision in *Brown v. Board of Education of Topeka*, not following Judge Davies's ruling ordering him to comply, and ignoring the orders of the president, Governor Orval Faubus was essentially obstructing justice—trying to impede or influence an action of the courts—according to executive order 10730. This is outlined in the introduction of the executive order. In part, it reads:

> *WHEREAS certain persons in the state of Arkansas, individually and in unlawful assemblages, combinations, and conspiracies, have willfully obstructed the enforcement of orders of the United States District Court for the Eastern District of Arkansas with respect to matters relating to enrollment and attendance at public schools, particularly at Central High School, located in Little Rock School District, Little Rock, Arkansas ...*

President Eisenhower was only the second president to use the medium of television to address the American public.

Having explained his reasons for taking action, President Eisenhower then discussed the actions he intended to take. There were four sections that outlined his course of action. First, he authorized the secretary of defense to order the National Guard and Air National Guard into Little Rock for as long as it took to resolve the crisis. Eisenhower had questioned originally whether or not to call in the National Guard since they would be expected to confront fellow members of the National Guard. He couldn't be sure that the troops would follow his orders. Therefore, he also called in the 101st Airborne Division, a force that was unquestionably loyal to the former World War II general.

In the second section, the president authorized the secretary of defense to use these troops to:

> *take all appropriate steps to enforce any orders of the United States District Court for the Eastern District of Arkansas for the removal of obstruction of justice in the State of Arkansas with respect to matters relating to enrollment and attendance at public schools in the Little Rock School District, Little Rock, Arkansas.*

Essentially, Eisenhower was ordering the governor of Arkansas to stand down and order the members of the Arkansas National Guard to also stand down, and allow the students to enter the school safely and attend classes. If the governor didn't comply, the secretary of defense could use force as he saw fit.

The third section read:

> *In furtherance of the enforcement of the aforementioned orders of the United States District Court for the Eastern District of Arkansas, the Secretary of Defense is authorized to use such of the armed forces of the United States as he may deem necessary.*

Here, the president was giving the secretary of defense permission to bring in more members of the armed forces, if necessary, to see that the court orders relating to integration were enforced.

The final section authorized the secretary of defense to confer and delegate responsibilities to the secretary of the army and secretary of the air force. This was essentially putting the secretary of defense in charge in case of any escalation or upheaval.

Finally, executive order 10730 was signed:

> *DWIGHT D. EISENHOWER*
> *THE WHITE HOUSE,*
> *September 24, 1957.*

The Country Reacts

The governor of Arkansas knew he was beaten and needed to stand down. However, he was not one to give up easily. In one last attempt to sway the president from taking military action, he asked the other members of the Southern Governors' Association to write letters to the president in solidarity with the Arkansas governor. These letters were released to the press around 6:30 p.m. on September 24, a little before Eisenhower would be addressing the nation about the situation in Little Rock and sharing his plan of action. The president went on air around 9:00 p.m., ignoring the letters and carrying on as planned.

In typical Eisenhower fashion, the president had chosen the words of the speech very carefully, explaining his reasons for action:

> *The very basis of our individual rights and freedoms rests upon the certainty that the president and the executive branch of government will support and insure the carrying out of the decisions of the federal courts, even, when necessary with all the means*

at the president's command. Unless the president did so, anarchy would result. There would be no security for any except that which each one of us could provide for himself. The interest of the nation in the proper fulfillment of the law's requirements cannot yield to opposition and demonstrations by some few persons. Mob rule cannot be allowed to override the decisions of our courts.

For many Southerners, Eisenhower's words were a bitter pill to swallow. In their eyes, this would overturn hundreds of years of "Southern custom." Put simply, white supremacy ruled in the South, and had for centuries. Integration would undermine institutionalized racism that had been accepted, even celebrated, for as long as the entire population of the South in the 1950s had been alive.

Eisenhower aide Ann Whitman noted the day after Eisenhower's speech that national reaction was divided neatly along the Mason-Dixon line—the fictional line that had divided the North and South in the years leading up to the Civil War—with mostly Southerners reacting negatively. But as a whole, 68.4 percent of the country (and 77.5 outside of the South) stood in support of the president's action in Little Rock.

The New Students

Melba Patillo, one of the Little Rock Nine, had just drifted off to sleep on the night of September 24 when she was awakened by loud voices. There were strange white men out on the porch, and having endured so much adversity and witnessed so much violence, Patillo's family were wary and afraid. Her grandmother

The Little Rock Nine were finally allowed to enter the school on September 23, 1957. Even under military protection, the students faced adversity.

even grabbed the shotgun and demanded to know what the men wanted. But they were soldiers, there representing the office of the president. They simply told Patillo that she should go back to school and would be protected in doing so.

On the morning of September 25, the crowd gathered again, but this time they were confronted by members of the National Guard who were there to protect the students, not the protestors. The angry crowd was quickly dispersed, with only one protestor suffering an injury—he tried to wrestle a bayonet from one of the service members. At last, with thirty soldiers accompanying them, the Little Rock Nine were allowed to enter the school safely. Around 10:00 a.m. a bomb threat was phoned in, leading to a short school evacuation. And around 750 white students skipped school that day. But the newest students at Central High reported that "everyone acted nice" and didn't run into any problems with the other students. Protests outside continued, but by the next morning, the protests seemed to be over.

Ruby Bridges Goes to School

Ruby Bridges is an icon of strength and determination.

Ruby Bridges became the first elementary student to be enrolled in an integrated school in the South on November 14, 1960. Six-year-old Bridges was escorted into William Franz Elementary School on the first day by federal marshals. Parents of white students immediately began pulling their children from school. One teacher, Barbara Henry, took on the task of teaching Bridges—the only student in an otherwise empty classroom. The other students' behaviors kept Bridges alone at lunchtime and recess.

By her second-grade year, however, Bridges was finally able to attend classes with other students. She even walked to school alone. After high school, Ruby Bridges went to business school and then went to work as a travel agent for American Express. A painting by Norman Rockwell, featuring Bridges, called *The Problems We All Live With*, hung on a wall at the White House during the Obama administration.

That evening, Governor Faubus addressed Arkansas citizens, saying, "We are now in occupied territory." The integration of Central High was only the first victory in a very long, very difficult war that would continue long after Eisenhower left office in 1961.

LITTLE ROCK CENTRAL HIGH SCHOOL

Chapter Three

The Order's Ongoing Legacy

One year after the integration of Central High School in Little Rock, Arkansas, Governor Orval Faubus closed the Little Rock public schools completely for the 1958–1959 school year. This time period is sometimes referred to in Arkansas history as "the Lost Year." Many white students who could afford the cost were simply sent to private schools.

That year, the members of the Little Rock Nine—except Ernest Green, who had graduated at the end of the previous school year—attended other schools or continued their education through correspondence. All went on to have amazing careers. Green came to work as an assistant secretary of the Department of Labor. Minnijean Brown worked in the Department of the Interior. Melba Patillo went to work as a

Opposite: Central High is now a historic site in Arkansas, allowing visitors to reflect on a significant time of crisis in US history.

reporter for NBC after earning her education. Gloria Ray received her bachelor's degree in chemistry and mathematics and worked as a systems analyst and patent attorney. Elizabeth Eckford served in the army for five years, and then went on to work as a history teacher and in state government. Thelma Mothershed became a teacher and later volunteered for the American Red Cross, teaching survival skills to homeless women. Terrence Roberts got a PhD in psychology and became a professor. Jefferson Thomas served in Vietnam and then worked as a civil servant for many years. (Thomas passed away in 2010.) Carlotta Walls became president of the Little Rock Nine Foundation, a scholarship organization, and founded a real estate brokerage firm.

However, what is the legacy of the executive order that finally forced school integration to take place in September 1957, and the president who issued it?

How We Remember Executive Order 10730

Ultimately, Eisenhower's executive order was a temporary fix to a situation that had deep roots and continues to plague America today. But one important note is that even though it was signed begrudgingly and more out of frustration against the Arkansas governor than a passion for human rights, this executive order helped to set the course for the Civil Rights Act of 1964 and the Voting Rights Act of 1965.

On June 23, 1958, Eisenhower met with civil rights leaders Martin Luther King Jr.; A. Philip Randolph of the Leadership Conference on Civil Rights; Roy Wilkins, the executive director of the NAACP; and Lester Granger, who headed the Urban

Although he was reluctant, Eisenhower met with civil rights leaders at the White House on June 23, 1958, including Martin Luther King Jr. (*second from left*).

League. At the time, this type of meeting was unprecedented, and even though Eisenhower felt frustrated that the leaders were not being "patient," as the president had suggested they do in a speech he had delivered in May, the issue was finally front and center for him. He promised the leaders that he would take action.

Civil rights were now at the forefront of American politics as the country prepared for the presidential election of 1960. Many of the American people wanted civil rights legislation. They wanted progress. Members of the Republican Party, including the president, could see that. The party had lost forty-eight seats to the more progressive Democrats in the House of Representatives and thirteen seats in the Senate in the 1958 elections. If the Republican Party wanted to gain a majority again, they had to prioritize civil rights. On December 10, 1958, Eisenhower announced his intention to allow the work of the Civil Rights Commission, founded in 1957 to help research, support, and promote important civil rights issues of the time, to continue as new issues came to light. Eisenhower did not have a perfect record when it came to civil rights, but he did believe in the Constitution and supported the rule of law, and that was what drove his actions.

On November 8, 1960, John F. Kennedy won the presidential election. Kennedy had run a campaign that supported civil rights. More than 70 percent of African American people voted

John F. Kennedy addressed the nation on June 11, 1963, in response to Alabama governor George Wallace fighting integration at the University of Alabama.

for Kennedy in that election, according to the John F. Kennedy Presidential Library. However, even Kennedy's more hands-on approach to the civil rights movement was not enough to put an end to racism in America. As the twentieth century came to an end and the twenty-first century began, the United States continued to struggle.

Segregation Continues

Although institutionalized school segregation is now illegal on the federal level, segregation still exists in many forms. One example of continued school segregation is due to American economics and employment discrimination. For decades, there has been a wage gap between black and white Americans. In 2015, the average hourly pay for a white person was $25.22, while the average black person made $18.49.

There is also discrimination within common hiring practices in the United States. Studies show that people with "black-sounding" names are not called in for job interviews as often as people with names more often associated with white people. It's simply harder to make a living as an African American citizen. Also, poorer Americans tend to live in less affluent neighborhoods and send their children to public schools in those neighborhoods. Schools in poorer neighborhoods tend to get less funding, resulting in a poorer education. According to an article in *Business Insider*, 37 percent of American public schools are attended by one race only.

Segregation also occurs because of tradition and a lack of effort in changing that tradition. Up until 2013, a high school in Wilcox County, Georgia, held separate proms for black and white students, privately organized by the students and their

Mareshia Rucker (*left*) and Stephanie Sinnot (*right*) were two of the four Wilcox County high school students who fought to have an integrated prom in 2013.

parents. Finally, in 2013, the school sponsored a prom to which all four hundred students were welcome. "Everything went off without a hitch," Wilcox County school superintendent Steve Smith said of the event. The 2009 documentary *Prom Night in Mississippi* is about a similar situation at Charleston High School in Charleston, Mississippi. The school integrated officially in 1970 but continued to hold separate proms for black students and white students. Actor Morgan Freeman grew up in the nearby town of Greenwood and in 1997, he offered to pay for the prom if everyone was allowed to attend. His offer was accepted eleven years later, and the event was captured for the documentary.

The final way that school segregation has been allowed to continue is through actual continued school segregation. In the town of Cleveland, Mississippi, up until 2017, the school district was involved in an ongoing court battle against segregation, which allowed Cleveland High to continue accepting predominantly white students and East Side High, mostly black students. In 2015, there were 180 school districts in the United States still fighting integration in court—44 of these in Mississippi alone. For years, Cleveland, Mississippi, schools offered a "freedom of choice" plan, which allowed students to decide for themselves where to enroll as negotiations continued between the justice department and the school district. Finally, in January 2017, they reached a settlement. The schools went to work hiring new principals and coming up with new mascots and colors for the new schools in order to help change the public perception of each school and make students feel comfortable attending.

And Furthermore

The Civil Rights Act of 1964 was originally proposed by President John F. Kennedy and signed into law after his death by his successor, Lyndon B. Johnson. This law outlawed racial discrimination within schools, restaurants, hotels, and other public services, and enforced equal access to employment. While this bill was not a perfect piece of legislation, it was the most comprehensive civil rights bill to date.

Race and Social Media Today

During the 1990s and 2000s, the World Wide Web was developed, changing everything: the way people communicate, the amount of information they are able to send and receive, and the spread of ideas. For the first time, people could connect with others across the globe through social media sites like Twitter and Facebook. News could spread instantly. People could share ideas and be a part of the discussion on politics, entertainment, culture, and more. But not all ideas are good ones and not all discussions lead to a better society. The internet has also been shown to help spread racist and white supremacist ideologies.

And Furthermore

Segregation has never been limited to African American students. In the decade preceding *Brown v. Board*, five Mexican-American families, whose children were being sent to separate underfunded "Mexican schools," filed suit in the case of *Mendez v. Westminster*. The families won the case before it advanced to the Supreme Court.

The National Policy Institute might sound like any ordinary think tank—an organization that gathers research and advocates for certain political issues and social causes—but beneath its ordinary-sounding name is a white supremacy organization that has grown and spread through social media and online forums like Reddit and 4chan. In the twenty-first century, a careful rebranding of white supremacy, racism, sexism, and xenophobia has given rise to the "alt-right" community entering the mainstream and finding its voice in American politics. And their ideas continue to spread. White supremacist "news" organizations are often used to spread fake or biased stories that drive fear and anger among readers—similar to ways that Jim Crow-era newspapers spread information that created fear, distrust, and anger against African Americans.

The Good News

Not all ideas are bad, however. The internet has also become a source of good, helping people share causes and spread awareness. For example, the internet has helped spread awareness about mental illness, transgender issues, and women's rights.

The "Me Too" movement, started by Tarana Burke (*far left*), grew through social media and the involvement of some high-profile celebrities.

Seeing Past Misconceptions About Black Lives Matter

Many opponents of the Black Lives Matter movement object on the grounds that "all lives" should matter. The truth is that, to BLM members, they do! The idea that the lives of black citizens matter does not mean that they matter *more* than the lives of everyone else, only that they should matter as much, especially in the media and the judicial system, which often shows bias toward white individuals.

For example, African American children represent between 33 and 38.5 percent of childhood abductions that take place in the United States each year, but they are often assumed by police to be runaways, rather than victims of a crime, according to Derrica Wilson of the Black and Missing Foundation. The media is also less likely to cover their disappearances. Black Lives Matter works to ensure that lives like theirs do not go unnoticed.

Social media has helped give voices to African American writers and activists, helping to spread the Black Lives Matter movement, a political movement created after the wrongful death of Trayvon Martin at the hands of George Zimmerman in 2013, who was acquitted of the crime. The organization was started by three women—Alicia Garza, Patrisse Cullors, and Opal Tometi—and has grown into a global network with forty chapters that fights against oppression and killings by police.

Patrisse Cullors, Opal Tometi, and Alicia Garza, shown here in 2016 receiving an award, founded the Black Lives Matter movement.

Social media has helped this kind of social awareness to spread in a way that could have helped better the lives of Homer Plessy and the other members of the Citizens' Committee, the Little Rock Nine, Rosa Parks, and centuries' worth of other American citizens who have faced oppression, discrimination, and violence.

Glossary

abolition The movement to end slavery in the United States.

boycott A refusal of the services of a business or organization by a large group of people used to express disapproval or force a change by that entity.

civil rights The basic rights of a citizen for personal freedom.

class-action lawsuit A civil case brought by a group of people who are suffering a similar injustice by the same company or individual.

clergy The collective leaders within a Christian religious organization.

conservative A political belief system based in tradition rather than progressive views.

emancipation A process by which an individual or group are given their freedom.

executive order A directive issued by the president (or governor, at the state level) that bypasses Congress, often in a case when urgency is required.

House of Representatives The chamber of Congress in which the number of representatives is determined by the number of districts within the state—more for states with higher population.

injunction An official order from court for a business, organization, or individual to refrain from performing a specific act.

integration The process through which more than one race are provided equal opportunities.

Jim Crow laws State laws, primarily in the southern United States, that were passed in order to restrict the freedoms of African American people, including former slaves after the Civil War.

legislation The action of creating laws within a democracy.

obstruction of justice A crime in which an individual or group works to influence, threaten, or interfere with an investigation or other part of the legal process.

plantation A large farm in the southern United States before the Civil War that grew crops like tobacco and cotton and relied on slave labor for production.

poll tax A fee required for voting, as a tool to restrict the voting rights of poorer citizens, primarily African Americans.

protest A public gathering of people intended to express disapproval with the intention of enacting change.

Reconstruction A period in the United States after which the Civil War had ended and the Southern states rejoined the Union.

secession An official act of gaining independence, as a state withdrawing from a nation.

segregation The separation of people by race.

Senate The chamber of Congress in which each state is represented equally.

slavery An institution by which people are owned by other people as property.

solidarity A spirit of unity.

telegram A message sent by a telegraph, a machine that transmitted messages via code through transmission wires.

tobacco A type of plant that is harvested for its leaves; used in the production of cigarettes, snuff, cigars, etc.

unconstitutional In violation of the US Constitution.

Further Information

Books

Beals, Melba Patillo. *Warriors Don't Dry: A Searing Memoir of the Battle to Integrate Little Rock's Central High.* New York: Simon Pulse, 2007.

Guelzo, Allen C. *Lincoln's Emancipation Proclamation: The End of Slavery in America.* New York: Simon and Schuster, 2006.

Henningfield, Diane Andrews. *Little Rock Nine.* Perspectives on Modern World History. Farmington Hills, MI: Greenhaven, 2014.

Smith, Jean Edward. *Eisenhower in War and Peace.* New York: Random House, 2013.

Williams, Juan. *Eyes on the Prize: America's Civil Rights Years, 1954–1965.* New York: Penguin, 2013.

Websites

The American Presidency Project

http://www.presidency.ucsb.edu/data/orders.php

This comprehensive database collects every recorded executive order in American history.

Dwight D. Eisenhower Presidential Library

https://www.eisenhower.archives.gov/about_us.html

The historic site houses the official paperwork and archives of President Dwight D. Eisenhower.

Kansas: *Brown v. Board of Education* National Historic Site

https://www.nps.gov/articles/brownvboard.htm

The National Park Service maintains an official visitor's center for Monroe Elementary School, the origin of the *Brown v. Board* case.

NAACP

http://www.naacp.org/oldest-and-boldest

This organization is the oldest and largest civil rights organization in the United States.

National Women's History Museum: Ruby Bridges

https://www.womenshistory.org/education-resources/biographies/ruby-bridges

This website explores the life and accomplishments of Ruby Bridges, as both a child and today.

Bibliography

Almasy, Steve, and Darran Simon. "A Timeline of President Trump's Travel Bans." CNN. March 30, 2017. http://www.cnn.com/2017/02/10/us/trump-travel-ban-timeline/index.html.

Black, Derek. "Why Schools Still Can't Put Segregation Behind Them." *Business Insider*. June 8, 2017. http://www.businessinsider.com/school-segregation-today-united-states-2017-6.

Doyle, Leonard. "Charleston's First Integrated Prom." *Independent*. June 12, 2008. http://www.independent.co.uk/news/world/americas/charlestons-first-integrated-prom-846261.html.

Eisenhower, Dwight D. "Executive Order 10730—Providing Assistance for the Removal of an Obstruction of Justice Within the State of Arkansas." The American Presidency Project. September 24, 1957. http://www.presidency.ucsb.edu/ws/index.php?pid=75572.

Garland, Sarah. "Was 'Brown v. Board' a Failure?" *Atlantic*. December 5, 2012. https://www.theatlantic.com/national/archive/2012/12/was-brown-v-board-a-failure/265939.

Gumbrecht, Jamie. "Georgia School Hosts First Racially Integrated Prom." CNN. April, 4, 2014. http://www.cnn.com/2014/04/04/living/integrated-prom-wilcox-county-georgia/index.html.

Harris, Paul. "How the End of Slavery Led to Starvation and Death for Millions of Black Americans."

Guardian. June 16, 2012. https://www.theguardian.com/world/2012/jun/16/slavery-starvation-civil-war.

History.com. "Emancipation Proclamation." History.com. http://www.history.com/topics/american-civil-war/emancipation-proclamation.

———. "Integration of Central High School." History.com. http://www.history.com/topics/black-history/central-high-school-integration.

———. "Reconstruction." History.com. http://www.history.com/topics/american-civil-war/reconstruction.

Klein, Rebecca. "Latino School Segregation: The Big Education Problem That No One Is Talking About." *Huffington Post*. October 26, 2015. https://www.huffingtonpost.com/entry/latino-school-segregation_us_561d70a5e4b050c6c4a34118.

Koba, Mark. "Executive Orders Coming? Here's How They Work." CNBC. January 28, 2014. https://www.cnbc.com/2014/01/28/executive-orders-what-they-are-and-how-they-work.html.

Mason, Heather. "Ruby Bridges and the New Orleans School Desegregation Crisis." Amy Poehler's Smart Girls. September 8, 2017. https://amysmartgirls.com/ruby-bridges-and-the-new-orleans-school-desegregation-crisis-14d8923dcc7a.

McNamara, Robert. "Ida B. Wells." ThoughtCo. March 6, 2016. https://www.thoughtco.com/ida-b-wells-basics-1773408.

National Park Service. "Jim Crow Laws." National Park Service. https://www.nps.gov/malu/learn/education/jim_crow_laws.htm.

Nichols, David A. *A Matter of Justice: Eisenhower and the Beginning of the Civil Rights Revolution*. New York: Simon and Schuster, 2008.

Office of the Historian. "The Declaration of Independence, 1776." Office of the Historian. https://history.state.gov/milestones/1776-1783/declaration.

OurDocuments.gov. "Plessy v. Ferguson (1896)." OurDocuments.gov. https://www.ourdocuments.gov/doc.php?flash=false&doc=52.

Prokop, Andrew. "How Republicans Went from the Party of Lincoln to the Party of Trump, in 13 Maps." Vox. November 10, 2016. https://www.vox.com/2016/7/20/12148750/republican-party-trump-lincoln.

Smith, Jean Edward. *Eisenhower in War and Peace*. New York: Random House, 2013.

United States Senate. "Freedmen's Bureau Acts of 1865 and 1866." United States Senate. https://www.senate.gov/artandhistory/history/common/generic/FreedmensBureau.htm.

———. "Landmark Legislation: Civil Rights Act of 1875." United States Senate. https://www.senate.gov/artandhistory/history/common/generic/CivilRightsAct1875.htm.

Vega, Tanzina. "Wage Gap Between Blacks and Whites Is Worst in Nearly 40 Years." CNN Money. September 20, 2016. http://money.cnn.com/2016/09/20/news/economy/black-white-wage-gap/index.html.

Index

Page numbers in **boldface** are illustrations.

About the Author

Bethany Bryan is the author of several books for Cavendish Square and Rosen Publishing, as well as an editor and copy editor for companies like Scholastic, Skyhorse, :01, and The Lion Forge. Her previous works include *The Cold War Chronicles: The Bay of Pigs and the Cuban Missile Crisis* and *Leading Women: Melania Trump: Model and First Lady*. She enjoys studying American history and visiting presidential museums, her favorite being Sagamore Hill in Oyster Bay, New York—the home of President Theodore Roosevelt. She lives in Kansas City, Missouri.